BRUCE JENNER

R. I. F.
(Reading Is FUNdamental)

BRUCE JENNER

by John Chodes & Gary Wohl

tempo
books

GROSSET & DUNLAP, INC.

Publishers New York

A FILMWAYS COMPANY

PICTURE CREDITS:
Cover: Don Chadez/Duomo
Gale Constable/Duomo: pages 30, 50, 69;
Duomo: page 82;
Graceland College: pages 13, 21, 25, 35, 74;
Bill Outhouse: page 10;
Paul J. Sutton/Duomo: pages 5, 22, 78, 83;
Steven E. Sutton/Duomo: page vi;
Wide World: pages 3, 47, 57, 67, 73, 76, 81, 86, 88.

ACKNOWLEDGMENTS
The authors wish to thank L.D. Weldon and Esther Jenner for
their kind help and cooperation in supplying us with so much
valuable background information.

We would also like to thank Myrna Morris of Graceland College,
Jim Schaeffler of ABC Sports, Rita Mennella, and Louis De Paul
of Newtown High School for their assistance.

For Shawn, Chico and Twiggy with thanks

CONTENTS

*After victory in the 1976 Olympic decathlon trial,
Bruce and admiring children are all smiles.*

CHAPTER ONE

THE GOLDEN HOUR

It was the next to the last day of the track and field events at the 1976 Montreal Olympic Games. A huge crowd filled the stadium. All day long they had cheered wildly as each exciting event produced one gold medal winner after another.

But now, as darkness crept over the stadium, a great new surge of emotion swept the crowd, unlike anything that had been seen or heard before. Most of the fans stood and roared. Along the backstretch of the track, someone waved a big American flag.

This sudden loud cheer was for Bruce Jenner as he jogged his victory lap after the painful 1,500-meter run, the tenth and final decathlon contest. Bruce Jenner had just won the gold medal, had broken the world record and would now be called "The World's Greatest Athlete."

While Bruce Jenner's rivals fell to the ground, gasping from total tiredness after all this, Bruce was so fresh and excited that he leaped and jumped and threw his hands way up in the air. He was so happy that he had won.

Suddenly Bruce saw his pretty wife, Chrystie, sitting in the

Bruce throws his hands up with happiness after breaking the Olympic and world decathlon record in the Montreal Olympics.

stands. Chrystie was so thrilled at Bruce's victory that she was crying. He ran to her and hugged and kissed her. "It's over now, it's over," he said, which meant that he had reached his goal, and now he could finally retire. He had spent the last eight years training for this moment.

Chrystie watched Bruce climb the victory stand, rising above Guido Kratschmer, the West German, who was second, and Nikolai Avilov, the third-place Russian. When Bruce was given his gold medal, he held it and kissed it. Chrystie was crying again . . .

The decathlon is the hardest of all the Olympic track and field events. In almost every other event, the answer to success is "specialize." The athelete spends years working on one kind of skill. For

Bruce taking his victory lap as the crowd cheers his triumph.

instance, the shot-putters have one arm that is often twice as large as the other arm because of all the extra training that it gets. The thinner arm and all the rest of the shot-putter's body are often weak compared to his one big arm.

Most runners have very strong legs but puny chests. The weight lifters have bulging muscles, but few of them can run more than a few blocks.

The decathlon man is different. He must be the master of a dozen different skills that strain every muscle in his body. He must develop talents that are supposed to be opposites: endurance and speed, strength and being limber.

"Decathlon" comes from the Greek word "deca," which means ten. The decathlon consists of ten contests in running, jumping, hurdling, vaulting and throwing, squeezed into two rugged days. Points are scored on how well the athlete does in each event. The man with the highest score is the champion.

At Montreal, Bruce Jenner was the Olympic decathlon champion. As he stood on the victory stand in front of those 75,000 live track fans and those millions more who watched him on television, Bruce Jenner sighed with relief. All the years of devotion could come to an end now. He had achieved his great dream.

But it had not been an easy road. His career had started ten years before, when he was in high school. As Bruce stood on the victory stand, ten years ago must have seemed more like a hundred years ago.

CHAPTER TWO

THE MOLDER

To Bruce, it seemed like a hundred years ago that he met L. D. "Jack" Weldon, the man who would change the entire course of his life. Weldon turned Bruce from a nobody into one of the most famous people in the world.

The meeting was so unlikely, Bruce could hardly believe that it happened the way it did. Jack Weldon was the athletic director for Graceland College, a small church school in Lamoni, a little town in southern Iowa. Jack Weldon had been a great athlete and then a famous coach for over 40 years. Way back when, Jack had been a super javelin thrower. (The javelin is a spear-throwing event. It was one of the original Olympic contests in the Greek Olympics thousands of years ago.) Jack had won the Big Ten championship twice (1929 and 1930), held the Amateur Athletic Union record (1928 and 1931) and had been a member of the American team that faced a British Empire team in 1931.

Then Jack began to coach. His record was amazing. He coached four men to world records and four others to N.A.I.A. decathlon national titles. (N.A.I.A. stands for the Na-

Bruce thanks his coach and friend L.D. Weldon after winning the Olympic decathlon gold medal.

tional Association of Intercollegiate Athletics.) His teams at Graceland won many regional titles.

But Jack Weldon's proudest moment was in coaching Jack Parker to a bronze medal (third place) in the decathlon at the 1936 Berlin Olympic Games. They had teamed up when Weldon was the track coach at Sacramento City Junior College. Parker was a student there. He could do anything. He was both a good football player and a track star. Weldon told Parker that his different talents were perfect for the decathlon. Parker was convinced. By coaching Parker, Weldon became one of the most famous decathlon coaches in America.

Lamoni, Iowa is not one of the biggest towns in America. Neither is Newtown, Connecticut. That is where Bruce went to high school. These two towns are 1,500 miles apart. How could Bruce Jenner and Jack Weldon find each other?

This is how. Jack Weldon had friends all over the United States looking for decathlon talent. One day he received a phone call from a coach who lived near Bruce. This man told Jack Weldon about a high school boy who was a one-man track team. This boy was a javelin thrower, a triple-jumper, a state champion in the pole vault and high jump. He was also a football player and a top-notch water-skier! This fellow was Bruce Jenner.

It wasn't hard to understand why Bruce was such a good athlete. He came from a family of sports-minded people. Years before, Bruce's grandfather Burton Jenner had been one of the top finishers in the famous long-distance foot race,

(Top) Bruce wearing number 10 leaps high to get a rebound during his high school days at Newtown. (Bottom) Bruce gets ready to shoot during a practice session at the Newtown High gym.

the 26-mile-long Boston Marathon. Bruce's father, Bill, was also an all-around sports nut. When Bill was a youngster, he played football and basketball, and he was a sprinter and a pole-vaulter, just like Bruce. When Bruce was a kid, his father set up a high-jump bar in the backyard. Bruce and his friends practiced jumping over it all the time.

Esther, Bruce's mother, was also very much into sports. When she was in school, she played volleyball and was an archer.

But there was one sport that the whole Jenner family did together, including his older sister, Pamela, and his younger brother, Bert. That sport was water-skiing. The Jenner family was crazy about it. They didn't just have fun at it. They entered water-ski meets and they all played to win.

From water-skiing Bruce learned to love the sports of one against one. In a team sport a man can blame other people for losing. In a one-man sport, like the decathlon, the glory or the blame cannot be put on someone else. Bruce liked the idea that winning and losing rested on his shoulders alone.

Bruce was born in 1949 in Ossining, New York. He and his family did a lot of moving around New York when he was a youngster. When Bruce was four, the Jenners moved to Cornwall-on-Hudson. That is where Bruce began school. At eight Bruce went to live in Yorktown Heights, in northern Westchester County. At 11 Bruce moved to Tarrytown, just above New York City. At around that point he began his water-skiing. By the time he was living in Newtown, Connecticut,

Bruce was 17 and a good athlete. Bruce met Jack Weldon when he was at Newtown High School.

Jack Weldon saw that Bruce's all-around talent for sports showed that he would be great for the decathlon. Bruce could triple-jump. That showed he had the spring in his legs to sprint and run the hurdles and the long jump. All these were decathlon events. Bruce was already a javelin thrower and a pole-vaulter. These were two more exciting contests in the decathlon.

Jack Weldon called Bruce at his home. "Son, how would you like to win a scholarship to Graceland College, where you could learn to be a decathlon man?"

Weldon held his breath. He was afraid that Bruce would answer, "The decathlon? Isn't that some sort of beauty contest?" That is what some boys had asked Weldon!

Instead, Bruce knew about the decathlon, and he was very interested. From there it took Jack Weldon only a few minutes to explain all about it and fill Bruce with the spirit for this hard sport.

But Weldon lured Bruce to make sure that he would come to Graceland. Weldon said that the scholarship would also be for football. Yet, once Bruce was at Graceland, Weldon knew he would do all that he could to change Bruce from football to the decathlon.

As for the scholarship, Bruce must have been a little disappointed. Graceland could not give him the free schooling, the big spending money, the free room and board that the bigger schools could offer. All that Graceland could give Bruce was a room to stay, at no cost. After a while this room would be in the basement of Jack Weldon's own home.

Still, Jack Weldon's high spirits spread to Bruce. Suddenly Bruce began to see a whole new sports career opening up for him. He grabbed hold of the decathlon idea right away, and he never let it go.

A few days after arriving at Graceland, Bruce dived right into the decathlon. "It is the greatest challenge there is. It has everything," Bruce said. But it seemed that one challenge was not enough. He had so much energy left that he also went into football and basketball. It seemed that Bruce could do everything and do it well, too.

Then—hardly after starting—disaster struck. In one of his first football games, Bruce was tackled very hard. Something cracked in his knee. Bruce was carried off the field.

The cartilage had been torn. This meant an operation. It might mean the end of both his football and his decathlon career before either one had really gotten off the ground.

Luckily the operation was a success. He healed perfectly. It wasn't too long before Bruce was training again. But even this bad injury wasn't a warning for Bruce to keep away from all sports except the decathlon. The hardest job that Jack Weldon had—and this would be true for several years—was to make Bruce stay with the decathlon and not fritter his time and energy away on a dozen different games. But Bruce loved all sports so much that he sometimes wanted to get into a football game or do some fast water-skiing just for the sheer fun of it, even when he was not in shape for it. But there were big dangers to fooling around this way, like getting hurt again. This wasn't so bad when Bruce first started out in the decathlon. But once he had spent years training for it . . . well . . . Jack Weldon would groan at the thought that all of Bruce's hard, hard work would go down the drain just because of another freakish injury from water-skiing or football or basketball.

Even with the warnings, Bruce was Bruce. His fun-loving nature could not be kept down. For instance, during Bruce's third year at Graceland, he went home to visit his family and entered the Eastern water-skiing championship. He slipped on a dangerous jump, fell into the water and badly twisted his "good" knee. It hurt him for a year, and he could not do his best during that whole time.

Bruce practices for the 110-meter hurdles race in the Graceland College gym.

Bruce competes in the 110-meter hurdles during the 1976 U.S. Olympic trials at Eugene, Oregon.

Although the decathlon is made up of ten different events, there are just three basic skills needed to be good at all the contests. One skill, the strength to sprint (to run very fast), is needed for five of the decathlon events: the 100 meters, the 400 meters (this is a quarter-mile sprint) and the 110-meter hurdle spring. Sprinting is even needed for the high jump and the long jump. Bruce learned that he could not jump high or long without being able to run very fast.

For the next four events, Bruce had to build up the strength in his arms, shoulders and back. These contests were the javelin (the spear throw) and the discus (a round weight throw). Also the pole vault and the shot put. This meant a lot of training in the gym, far from the track, on a weight machine.

The skills of sprinting and

arm strength were needed for nine decathlon events. The tenth contest was the 1,500 meter run. That is equal to one mile. A mile is a long way. To be able to finish it took another kind of skill: endurance. Endurance means not getting tired even after doing a hard exercise for a long time. To build endurance, Bruce had to run for miles and miles. It was very tiring, but there was no other way to build it.

Even after learning all these skills, Bruce was still not a decathlon man. This was just the beginning. Now he had to learn how to do each contest by itself. Each one was unlike every other. Each one had to be practiced over and over again.

Bruce felt scared. He had no idea that it would be so hard. There were so many things to learn. Jack Weldon understood Bruce's fears.

Bruce shows the correct way to hold the fiberglass pole as he starts his approach run in the pole vault. The knee brace supports the knee that was hurt in football.

He said that it would all make sense once Bruce trained in the right way. Then Weldon showed him how. Training would be broken up into three types of workouts. On the first day, Bruce would practice the first five events: the 100 meters, the long jump, the shot put, the high jump, the 400 meters. The next day, he would practice the other five: the 110-meter hurdles, the pole vault, the javelin, the discus, the 1,500 meters. He practiced them roughly in the same order that they would be held in the Olympics.

On the third day, Bruce would go to the gym and work out with weights. Then, the next day, he would start all over again. Sure, it sounds simple, but just to clear a hurdle without tripping and falling on his face took months for Bruce to learn well.

CHAPTER THREE

THE MUNICH OLYMPIC GAMES

In the spring of 1970, after his knee had healed, Bruce Jenner entered his first decathlon meet. It was at the famous Drake Relays track meet.

Bruce did very well for a first-time try. He was sixth. He scored 6,991 points. This was a Graceland College record. Jeff Bennet, one of the best decathlon men in the country, won with a great point score of 8,072. That was not so far behind the world record of 8,417, which was set by Bill Toomey, the 1968 Olympic champion.

The next time out, at the N.A.I.A. championships, Bruce took third place. Jeff Bennet won this one too.

The next spring, Bruce showed how fast he was improving. He won the Kansas Relays and the N.A.I.A. championships and was second in the Drake Relays. Even in this loss he reached his highest point score: 7,458.

The year 1972 was Bruce's last one in college. This was a very important and exciting time. When he won the Drake Relays decathlon, Bruce qualified for the Olympic trials, which would be held at Eugene, Oregon.

This was the biggest moment in Bruce's life. It was something he had always dreamed of—to have the chance to be on the American Olympic team. Bruce trained harder than ever.

"Well coach, do you think I can make it?" Bruce asked Jack Weldon just before the Olympic trials began.

"Bruce, I'll be truthful," Jack Weldon answered. "You have an outside chance if you have a real good day."

Then the trials began. Bruce started out by not having such a good day. His weakest events were held on that first day, and he looked weaker than usual. He was not very good on that first day because he was not a very good sprinter, and that was the day for all the high speed events: the 100 meters, the 400 meters and the high jump. He was weak in the shot put. He had never even thrown it once before coming

to Graceland. Yet Bruce had to face all these hard tests on the first day.

Bruce was better in the second day's events because he had years of practice with the javelin and the pole vault from his high school days.

Bruce was 11th in points at the end of the first day. That was not encouraging. Only the three highest point scores would be on the American Olympic team going to Munich, Germany.

Bruce was discouraged. He was nervous. The big crowds and the pressure to do well caused him to make mistakes. This was costing him points. But there was still a slight chance to make the team.

Then came the second day. That is when Bruce began to show what he could do. He began to do

Bruce clearing the high-jump bar. This was never one of his strongest events.

very well, picking up points like crazy and steadily catching the leaders.

After the ninth event, the javelin throw, Bruce looked up at the scoreboard. He was dead tired. He was sure that his Olympic dream was over. He was just too far behind the leaders.

Suddenly the scoreboard gave the point scores. His last few really good efforts had brought him up from 11th into fifth place. And . . . the difference between fifth and third place was not too great. And . . . third place meant a place on the Olympic team.

Just the thought of how close he was made Bruce super-excited. "I never felt like that before," he said later. "I jumped and yelled, 'I can do it!' I was pumped! A mile high! I went totally crazy!" His heartbeat raced as fast as it did when he ran hard for miles. "The trainer was trying to calm me down, and I was sitting on the training table, crying. I thought, 'Oh my God, Jenner, you're falling apart!'"

Steve Gough and Fred Samara were the men in third and fourth place. Bruce had to knock them off to make the Olympic team. They all came to the starting line for the last event: the 1,500-meter run. Bruce had to run the race of his life to have a chance. And . . . he did! The crowd, his own excitement, everything worked. Bruce ran like a madman and broke his own fastest time by eight full seconds! He crushed Gough and Samara. Bruce's wild run gave him 7,846 points. He was third! He joined Jeff Bennet and Jeff Bannister on the Olympic team. He made it! He hugged Jack Weldon right in the middle of the track, he was so happy.

Bruce ran to the nearest telephone. He called his parents back home. He made sure that his mom and dad were on the phone before he told them the great news. But he was still breathing hard from the 1,500-meter run, so they could hardly hear him. "Guess what folks, your son has just made the Olympic team!" His parents were just as thrilled as he was.

Years later, before the Montreal Olympics, when he was asked about that wonderful moment, Bruce answered, "Even if I win the gold medal in Montreal, I really believe that will be the greatest thrill I will ever have in track and field. Nobody expected me to do it. I didn't expect to do it."

The 1972 Munich Olympic Games. Thousands of the best athletes in every sport came there, hoping to win a gold medal. Bruce

Bruce battles Jeff Bennet. Both made the 1972 Olympic decathlon team.

trained as hard as he could, but he could not fool himself. He knew that he did not have a chance in the world to win the Olympic decathlon gold medal. The Russians had two great men. Their names were Avilov and Litvinenko. There were great Germans and many top men from other East European countries. Even the two other Americans, Bannister and Bennet, had a chance for a medal.

But . . . the excitement of the Olympics does strange things to great athletes. It gets some men so hopped-up (like Bruce in the trials) that they do better than ever before —or—they become so scared and psyched-out that they do far worse than they should. This second thing is what happened to Bruce Jenner. He was in top shape, but each time he looked up at the huge crowds in the stands, his knees started shaking and then he couldn't do anything well.

Maybe he was also nervous because his parents had come all the way to Munich to watch him. Mrs. Jenner had seen many of Bruce's decathlon meets in the U.S.A. Later she said, "At first the Munich Olympic Games seemed just like an ordinary track meet but when BRUCE JENNER, U.S.A. flashed on the scoreboard, I realized that this really was the Olympics, and I started trembling."

The Russian Nikolai Avilov loved the crowds, and he did even better when they cheered him. He smiled and waved back at them. They turned him on. It did not take long to see that no one would come close to beating Avilov. He was not only sure to win the gold medal, but he was also piling up so many points that he set a new world record of

8,454 points. He beat the other Russian, Litvinenko, by over 400 points! That was an unbelievable lead.

It had not been so many years before that people had said no one could ever break the 8,000-point barrier. It was supposed to be beyond any man's strength. Then in 1960, Rafer Johnson became the first man in the Olympics to crash through that "magic" barrier with a score of 8,392.

Bruce Jenner tried as hard as he could, but his nerves let him down. He scored only 7,722 points. That was lower than in the Olympic trials. Bruce finished tenth. That discouraged Bruce but not Jack Weldon. Jack knew that if Bruce studied why he had failed, he could learn a whole lot from his mistakes. And if Bruce took to heart what he learned, Jack felt that there was a chance that in four years, at the

Montreal Olympics, Bruce might have a chance to win a third-place bronze medal. Anything better than that would be too good to expect ever.

Bruce had to learn two important things from his defeat at Munich. He had to learn not to be afraid of the big crowds and the pressure of the Olympics. And just as important, Jack Weldon made Bruce see that the Russian Avilov had won not because he was a superman but because he understood how to be consistent. Consistent means being steady, being even. Avilov won only three of the ten decathlon contests. Yet, even in the seven that he lost, he was close to the leaders. That way he was still building up valuable points.

But Bruce had been like a yo-yo. In a few events he had finished near Avilov. In the javelin throw Bruce finished second. That was terrific. But when Bruce did poorly, he did very, very poorly. In the 100-meter sprint he was 24th. In the shot put, 22nd. In the long jump, 30th.

Avilov showed the right way to be the best: Don't train to be greater in your best event. Instead, improve your weakest events.

Bruce had not been beaten so badly that he wanted to quit. In fact, the opposite was true. Secretly he had made a big decision. He would devote himself for the next four years to becoming the best decathlon man in the world. He would try to win the gold medal at the Montreal Olympics.

Until the 1972 Olympics, Bruce had it fairly easy. He had no worries except homework and passing his classes. And, of course, practicing for the decathlon.

After the Munich Olympics everything changed. And it was not for the better. Suddenly Bruce was graduating from college. In school he had studied to be a gym teacher. Now he would have to go out and work full-time to earn a living. There would be hardly any time or energy left after a hard day of work to train at all, much less to try even harder for an Olympic gold medal. It seemed certain that his dream could never come true.

CHAPTER FOUR

CHRYSTIE'S BIG SACRIFICE

But all was not lost. Between all his sports and school activities, Bruce had found the time to fall in love and get married. And his wife, Chrystie, had the answer that lead Bruce to the Olympic gold medal. It happened this way: In high school and even in college, Bruce had never been a big social butterfly. He dated some girls, but most of his time and energy went into sports. "Besides," he complained, "girls. are too expensive." It cost money to date and Bruce wasn't exactly rich.

For the first three years at Graceland, Bruce did not meet one girl that he could call "extra special." But in 1972, in his senior year, his parents had a big surprise. They traveled to the Drake Relays to watch Bruce compete. There they met a "special friend" of his. This friend was a beautiful blond student from Graceland. She was a minister's daughter all the way from San Jose, California. Her name was Chrystie.

Mom and Dad Jenner knew, just from the way that Bruce looked at Chrystie, that she was more than just a friend. It wasn't too long before Bruce and Chrystie were married.

Bruce often told Chrystie of

all his secret dreams about winning the Olympic gold medal. He told her how hopeless it seemed, with his having to work and all.

But Chrystie was a smart girl. She understood how much it meant to Bruce to have another chance in the Olympics. She thought of a plan. It was daring, and it meant she would have to make a big sacrifice. But she was willing. Chrystie explained it to Bruce. She would quit school for a while and go to work to support both of them. If Bruce did not have to work, he could be a full-time athlete.

Chrystie knew that this would be hard on her. It meant working for four straight years—not for something that would be theirs together but for Bruce's glory. That is a hard sacrifice to make, but she was glad to do it.

Chrystie became an airline

stewardess. The airlines were looking for pretty, smart girls like her. It wasn't long before she had her uniform and was flying.

All this was great for Bruce. This was the kind of life he needed to become the best in the world. And what a difference it made! Bruce was able to double his training time. Instead of four hours, he practiced six or seven hours a day. Training became his full-time job. It was not only twice as long, but Bruce was doing much more thinking and planning than ever before.

As his way of thanking Chrystie for her sacrifice, Bruce promised her that, win or lose, he would retire right after the Montreal Olympics. Then she could pick up her schooling where she had left off, and he would go to work.

Bruce's most important plan was to spend most of his time improving each weakness, like his form in the 110-meter hurdles. Sometimes he would trip over them and lose lots of time. He also had to improve his slow sprinting speed.

Bruce was also too skinny to be a great shot-putter. He weighed 195 pounds. Most top shot-put men look more like football linemen. They weigh around 250 to 300 pounds.

Day after day Bruce was out at the track doing sprint starts to make his legs move faster and faster. He spent hours more in the gym, on the weight machine, building up his arms. Maybe he couldn't be as strong as a 300 pounder, but he certainly was going to try to be the best 195-pound shot-putter in the world!

Bruce poses with his wife, Chrystie, and their pet dog, Bertha.

CHAPTER FIVE

TWO LONELY YEARS

Practicing seven hours a day is hard even to think about. ·But to do it is much, much worse. More than hard, it was lonely.

The loneliness of missing Chrystie made each seven-hour workout seem like seven days. Bruce began to wonder if it was all worth it. Often Bruce's only training companion was his big St. Bernard dog, Bertha. Bertha would trot beside Bruce during his morning run. It was nice having Bertha next to him, but she was no fun to talk to. Bertha never answered back!

Then the lonely, cold Iowa winters gave Bruce a great idea. It was so hard to practice in that wind and snow. So he decided to go half-way across the country, to California, to the town of San Jose. This was the place where Chrystie's parents lived. Bruce knew he would really miss all his friends at Grace-land, especially Jack Weldon, who had been such a great help and inspiration. But Bruce had to go.

It would be a great help to live in California. The climate was warm all year around. That meant that Bruce could train outdoors through all four seasons.

Just as important, the warm weather had brought thousands of other track men to California. That

meant there were track meets almost every week of the year. Bruce needed lots of meets to keep sharp and to measure his improvement. Suddenly this gave Bruce another terrific idea.

Bruce must have said to himself: "When I am on the West Coast, I will be able to train and race against the guys who are the best in their own event. I know I will seem like a fool against them, but look at all I will learn about style, about training, about doing it better. If I throw the discus with Mac Wilkins or the shot put with Al Feuerbach, they will still be 20 feet ahead of me. They are the best at their game, but I will learn so much more."

So Bruce moved to San Jose with Chrystie and competed against

Bruce improved his shot-putting when he moved to San Jose.

the best men, not just the best decathlon men. And little by little it paid off. Bruce improved. Then he improved some more, but he still had a long way to go to make headlines. But he was serious. The decathlon was always on his mind, when he was awake and even while he was sleeping.

There was a hurdle right in the middle of his living room. Instead of going around it, Bruce would jump over it. And at night . . . it had always been hard on Bruce when Chrystie was away flying, but it was just as hard on her when she returned . . . without knowing it, Bruce kept waking her up all during the night. Chrystie said: "He actually practices events in his sleep. His legs move. He throws the shot put. He runs in his sleep. If he runs for ten seconds, I know he's running the 100 meters."

CHAPTER SIX

THE GREAT BREAKTHROUGH

Suddenly it all began to come together. Bruce opened the 1974 track season with a great win in the Kansas Relays track meet. His decathlon score was 8,240 points. It was the first time that Bruce had gone over the 8,000-point barrier in his life. This victory was followed by an even better one two months later. Bruce became the Amateur Athletic Union (A.A.U.) champion with 8,245 points. With these two victories he became a famous athlete. He was selected to represent the U.S.A. in a decathlon meet in Estonia, which is part of Russia. It was a team meet. America was fighting Russia and West Germany.

Bruce scored a big upset by winning with the highest score of his life: 8,308 points. His high score made it possible for the whole American team to win the meet.

This was the first time that Bruce had been on a foreign athletic trip since the Munich Olympics. The meet took place in Tallin, the capital of Estonia. Before the meet Bruce was just like an ordinary tourist. He enjoyed walking through the city and meeting the people, seeing the strange buildings and odd way everyone dressed and talked. It was unlike anything back home.

Bruce's score at Tallin was the fourth highest in history. And it was only the second time in history that one man hit over 8,000 points three times in one year. Only Bill Toomey, the 1968 Olympic champion, had done it before.

And Bruce was only 142 points behind Avilov's world record of 8,454. That may sound like a big difference, but it really isn't. All that Bruce needed to do to break the record was to make small improvements in each of the ten events.

Suddenly Bruce realized that he really could do it! He figured it out. By just building up steadily for one more year, he could do it. With this tough goal to shoot for, Bruce trained harder than ever.

Exactly one year later, in August, 1975 in Eugene, Oregon, Bruce did it! On the same track where he had qualified for the Munich Olympics, he set a great new world record: 8,524 points. What made it more wonderful was that it was set in a meet where he battled Nikolai Avilov, the Munich Olympic champion. Bruce crushed him and took away the Russian's world record at the same time.

As soon as the meet was over, Bruce ran to a phone and called both his parents and Jack Weldon. He had to share the news. Everyone was very happy. But then they all knew that Bruce could do it. It took days for Bruce to come down from the thrill of his world record. He had worked for years for it, and once he got it, it was awfully hard to feel normal.

Chrystie tells the story of what happened then. "I don't think the full impact of breaking the world record hit Bruce for a day

Chrystie hugs Bruce after he set the world decathlon record at Eugene, Oregon.

or two. For the next couple of nights, he kept waking me up and saying, 'Congratulations Chrystie,' and kissing me. I guess he did it because he figured he couldn't congratulate himself.''

Two months after his world record, Bruce entered the Pan-American Games. Only the Olympics are more important. There were the same big crowds and the same excitement as at the Olympics.

The reporters and the fans expected Bruce to do it again, to set another world record. They wanted something super. But they were shocked at what really happened. Bruce almost lost. He was just able to win the gold medal, but it was very, very close. And his point score was far short of the world record. Fred Dixon, another American, almost beat Bruce. It was much too close for comfort. People began to say, "Bruce Jenner is finished. He has passed his peak. He will never be the same again."

To outsiders this is the way it looked. But the real story was very different. In fact, Bruce hardly trained at all for the Pan-American Games. Right after he set the world record, he cut his training down so that he was almost loafing. It wasn't that he was washed up. He was taking a rest to get himself ready for his one last great buildup—the buildup that would prepare him for the Montreal Olympic Games. Bruce hoped that he had stored up enough strength to win the Pan-American Games without really training hard for them. His plan worked but not by much. In fact, Fred Dixon was in front all the way, for nine of the ten events. Bruce once again had to roar from behind in the 1,500 meters, and he just squeeked by to win. Bruce had 8,045 points. Dixon had 8,019.

Bruce felt lucky as he stood on the victory stand with his gold medal, listening to the Star-Spangled Banner play and the cheers of the huge crowd. His gold medal had almost become a silver medal. Silver is for second place.

Now Bruce began to train for his final decathlon. After the Olympics he would retire. By the time of the Olympic Games, he would have been training and competing for eight years. Win or lose, he had promised Chrystie that he would quit. But Bruce was not all that sure about his chances in the Olympics. He was afraid that Avilov would make a strong comeback and win again. Avilov was a great veteran and one of the toughest men in the world. He would not let Bruce win easily at Montreal.

CHAPTER SEVEN

THE LAST GREAT BATTLE

Bruce could not allow himself to get a swelled head by thinking he could not lose the Olympic gold medal. Of course, he held the world record, but whenever he felt too sure of himself, Bruce would remember what happened just one month before his world record.

It had happened in the National Championship meet. As usual, Bruce was doing fine in the decathlon, until he reached the pole vault. Suddenly he fouled up his approach run. His feet got tangled up so badly that he couldn't do the vault at all. Later, he said, "I yelled a curse as loud as I could right on national TV. Then I winged my pole as far as I could and just kept running. I ran out of the stadium, ran out through a field, sat under a clump of trees and just cried my eyes out. It was the only time I ever lost control in a meet."

Just thinking about this disaster made Bruce train harder to beat Avilov all the more.

Then, once again, it was time for the Olympic trials. Bruce was more than ready. He was at his peak. He set another world record! This time it was 8,538 points. He came to Montreal all primed for the final, greatest battle of his life.

On July 30, 1976, the Olympic decathlon began. The crowds were bigger than ever. These were the same mobs of people that had scared Bruce to death in Munich. But now Bruce had learned to love them, to respond to their cheers and not to be afraid of them. Now all the cheers turned him on.

Waiting for the battle to begin was the hardest part. Later Chrystie told reporters: "It's the waiting that has been so tough, the agony of waiting for it to be over. The day before he competed, we went up to St. Adele, a beautiful little ski area an hour from here. It was wonderful. Peace and quiet. Heavenly quiet. No one to bother you. But Bruce couldn't even get away from it there. He picked up a stick and threw it, pretending it was a javelin. We were standing on a dock, and he started going through his discus motions. I was trying to act calm and cool, but I really was very scared inside. I think I faked it pretty good."

There was a lot of pressure on Bruce, not just to win for himself, but to help the whole American team. They had not been doing very well. Bruce shared an apartment with 12 top American athletes. They included Dave Roberts and Earl Bell, two great pole-vaulters, and John Powell, the fine discus man from San Jose. Also there was Henry Marsh, the steeplechaser, and the other two men on the decathlon team; Fred Samara and Fred Dixon. It would not have been too much to expect a whole handful of gold and silver medals from this group. But no. They didn't even win one gold or silver medal. So, one of Bruce's roommates said to him, "Bruce, it looks like you are going to have to carry us now." It was up to Bruce to win a medal. That made the pressure to win ever greater. He had to win for all of them.

The first day of the battle gave a good idea of what was going to happen. Avilov had improved slightly in a few events, but he had also fallen behind what he had done in Munich in several others. In points at the end of the first day, Avilov was actually behind his old Olympic record.

In the many months of planning for this moment, Bruce had figured that he would be around 200 points behind Avilov at the end of the first day. Avilov's strongest events were on the first day. Bruce knew that this meant he would have to struggle like crazy on the second day if he were going to have a chance to win.

But now in the real fight, the points showed how much Bruce

had improved. Instead of being 200 points behind, he was breathing down Avilov's neck. Bruce was only 17 points behind the Russian. Then suddenly a new man, a new threat, appeared. The West German Guido Kratschmer zoomed past both of them. He led Bruce by 35 points.

Now Avilov was nervous—too nervous. He knew it was going to be a tough battle. In the 100 meters he made a false start. That means he began running before the starter's gun went off. That was bad. Two false starts and Avilov would be out of the race for good. So he had to be careful. That made him run the 100 meters much more slowly than usual. Bruce's 100-meter time was faster. This had never happened before. Usually Avilov was a much better sprinter.

But in the 400 meters, Bruce

Bruce shows the strain as he wins his heat of the 400 meters. His teammate Fred Dixon wears number 919.

made one of the best improvements of his whole career. At Munich four years before, Avilov had whipped Bruce by a full second: 48.5 seconds to 49.5 seconds. Now at Montreal, Avilov was razor sharp. He flew around the track and cut his time down to 48.2. That was a strong improvement.

Yet the big crowd was stunned by Bruce's race. He cut two full seconds from his best time at Munich, hitting 47.5 seconds. That was unbelievable. Improvements are usually measured in tenths of seconds. This means that the Bruce of Montreal would have beaten the Bruce of Munich by nearly 20 yards. Bruce burned Avilov right into the dust.

Then there was another hint of what was going to happen. A few

Even in a big meet, Bruce has a sense of humor. Notice what it says on his shirt.

months before the Olympics, Bruce had injured his left hand, and it was so painful that he could not throw the shot put at all. Bruce was very worried about this. Just before the Olympic Games, his hand started feeling better. He threw the shot put nearly 48 feet in his last workout. That would be just enough to get by. But in the real Olympic shot put on his third throw, he tossed the 16-pound ball over 50 feet. This was his best throw ever. It was nearly two feet longer than Avilov's best. That is when Bruce said to himself, "Three personal records in a row. I know I am headed for a big meet."

Then came the next event. "I was shooting for 6 feet 8 inches in the high jump. I made it, an inch over the best I'd ever done. That meant four big events in a row. I'd never done that before."

Later he said, "After that first

day I felt the greatest I've ever felt. I was shocked at how well I was doing."

Then it was the second day and the final five events. The struggle was getting tougher, but it didn't change Bruce's big sense of humor. Between contests he wore his own warm-up shirt, which certainly was not part of the American team's equipment. On his shirt in bold letters, it said, "Feet, don't fail me now."

Bruce now felt that he could beat Avilov and Kratschmer—until the 110-meter hurdle race. This race takes perfect timing and lots of sprinting speed. It was in this race that Bruce almost lost his hopes for a gold medal. One stumble over a hurdle could mean falling on his face, and that would be the end of the whole thing. Bruce had been very shaken up when he saw this happen to his old rival and team-mate Fred Dixon. Dixon was right in the thick of the fight when he stumbled on a hurdle. He nearly fell down and he lost four seconds. That one mistake put Dixon out of the picture to win a medal.

That is why Bruce decided to take the hurdles race very easily. He must have said to himself, "Better to finish a little slower and do it right than run crazy, fall down and lose a ton of points."

Bruce followed that plan. But in going easy, he lost ground to Avilov and Kratschmer. Bruce was now in trouble again, and just when he thought he had it won. To win the gold medal, he would have to be at his very best in the last four events.

The miracle began in the seventh and eighth events: the discus and the pole vault. This was the

After throwing the discus for years, Bruce's arms have really developed.

homestretch. Now Bruce revived. He had to, and he did.

Bruce threw the discus 164 feet, 16 feet farther than at Munich. Avilov was falling apart. He lost five feet from his best throw at Munich. Bruce was adding points and closing in.

Avilov felt the pressure and became more afraid. Avilov was always known to be cool. He never became shook-up by the big pressure of big-time sports. But with the Olympic gold medal riding on every move, he began to make mistakes—from fear. Now the whole decathlon began to turn around.

The next miracle occurred in the pole vault. It is a frightening— and a dangerous—event. It takes courage to leap over the crossbar more than 15 feet in the air. When

Bruce uses all his strength vaulting over the bar.

*Bruce throws the javelin. This event was in the origi-
nal Greek Olympics 2,000 years ago.*

a person is flying up there, 15 feet can look and feel like a thousand feet up. Bruce was the only one who was not afraid of that height. He equaled the highest vault of his life: 15 feet 9 inches. He made mincemeat out of Avilov and Kratschmer. Bruce was right back in the thick of the fight. In fact, when the pole vault was over and the points added up, Bruce Jenner found that he was in the lead!

Bruce was thrilled. He always had a good attitude whether he was winning or losing. When a reporter asked Bruce if he hated his opponents, he replied, "Hate them? I love them. They bring out the best in me." That is what was happening here in Montreal.

The ninth event. The javelin. He threw it eight feet farther than at Munich four years before. It was one of the best throws of his life.

But now the pressure to beat Bruce was killing Avilov. His best throw was eight feet shorter than at Munich. Even Kratschmer threw better than that. But not as far as Bruce. Bruce was pulling away from both of them.

There was a half-hour break between the javelin and the tenth and final event, the 1,500-meter run. "I looked up at the stands and looked around at all the people. It would be my last decathlon. I'd decided long before that I would quit, but I was beginning to realize now what that meant. I told myself that the 1,500 meters coming up was the last race I would ever run. I got a little choked up. I cried a few tears."

The 1,500-meter run. Avilov and Kratschmer still had one last chance to pull it out. But the whole

The 1,500-meter run, the last event in the Montreal Olympic decathlon. Bruce is about to pass his arch rival, Nikolai Avilov.

decathlon blew apart for them in this race. After two long, long days, this one-mile run must have seemed more like a 26-mile marathon.

Everything would be decided now. Each man ran his heart out. The four laps of the track were really painful. Avilov and Kratschmer started off fast, but after two laps the awful strain of the whole ten events ripped them apart. They couldn't move fast anymore. But Bruce took off like a rabbit and ran the fastest 1,500 meters of his life. He ran each lap faster than the one before.

The 75,000 people in the stadium were suddenly on their feet screaming. Bruce's mother was shouting and crying at the same time. As soon as she realized that the gold medal was his, as Bruce was straining for the finish line,

Bruce proudly waves the American flag as he jogs his victory lap after winning the Olympic decathlon.

(Above) Bruce shakes hands with Avilov while wait-ing to receive his gold medal. Kratschmer looks on. (Opposite page) Bruce's excitement on the victory stand is obvious as he shows off his gold medal.

Mrs. Jenner thought to herself, "Bruce honey, you just got everything you ever dreamed of."

Bruce sprinted the last yards to the finish line, threw his hands up in the air and shouted with joy! His time of 4:12 clinched the gold medal. The fast time added so many extra points that Bruce, for the third time, set a new world record: 8,618 points! The crowd continued roaring. They waved American flags.

As many of the decathlon men crossed the finish line, they dropped to the ground, gasping and half dead from being so, so tired. But Bruce had a big smile on his face as he began his victory lap. He saw Chrystie sitting in the stands. He rushed over to her and held her in his arms and said, "It's over now. It's over."

CHAPTER EIGHT

THE FUTURE

The Olympics were over. Bruce Jenner was a worldwide hero. As he promised Chrystie, he retired. But instead of it being the end of his career, his new fame started a whole new life.

A big publicity company managed Bruce. They held a news conference and invited reporters to interview him. Naturally, one reporter asked Bruce about his future

Home again, Bruce shows Chrystie and his mom and dad his Olympic gold medal.

plans. Bruce answered that he wasn't sure what he would do yet. "I'm so thrilled. I'm just riding high on the wind right now. But I've had a lot of requests in the last few days."

Bruce put his arms around Chrystie. "ABC has talked to me about speaking during atheltic events, and NBC has talked to us." (Soon ABC also hired Bruce and Chrystie to talk on their "A.M. America" morning TV show.) Bruce also added that he had several offers to play movie roles, including the main part in a film called "Superman."

"I'm just thinking it all over and I'm open for suggestions. First, Chrystie and I are taking off for a vacation in Hawaii. We are going to slow down. I've trained very hard for ten years. It's time to dedicate myself to something else."

Bruce is welcomed at his parents' house as a hero
by neighborhood youngsters.

A reporter asked Chrystie if she felt bad about supporting Bruce through the last four years.

"No. I'm really a happy lady. It was a good sacrifice. Everyone keeps looking at him like he's a superstar, and they gave us a big hotel room here. But we look to each other like the same old people. He's still Bruce."

OLYMPIC DECATHLON WINNERS

1912:	Hugo Wieslander, Sweden	5,377 points
1920:	Helge Lovland, Norway	5,190 points
1924:	Harold Osborn, U.S.A.	6,163 points
1928:	Paavo Yrjola, Finland	6,246 points
1932:	James Bausch, U.S.A.	6,588 points
1936:	Glenn Morris, U.S.A.	7,310 points
1948:	Bob Mathias, U.S.A.	6,386 points
1952:	Bob Mathias, U.S.A.	7,887 points
1956:	Milton Campbell, U.S.A.	7,937 points
1960:	Rafer Johnson, U.S.A.	8,392 points
1964:	Willi Holdorf, Germany	7,887 points
1968:	Bill Toomey, U.S.A.	8,193 points
1972:	Nikolai Avilov, U.S.S.R.	8,454 points
1976:	Bruce Jenner, U.S.A.	8,618 points

BRUCE JENNER'S OLYMPIC RESULTS

	MUNICH 1972 OLYMPIC GAMES	MONTREAL 1976 OLYMPIC GAMES
First day events:		
100-meter run:	11.3 seconds	10.9 seconds
Long jump:	21 feet 5 inches	23 feet 8 $1/_4$ inches
Shot put:	44 feet 6 inches	50 feet 4 $1/_4$ inches
High jump:	6 feet 3 $1/_2$ inches	6 feet 8 inches
400-meter run:	49.5 seconds	47.5 seconds
Second day events:		
110-meter hurdles:	15.6 seconds	14.8 seconds
Pole vault:	14 feet 11 $1/_4$ inches	15 feet 9 inches
Javelin:	216 feet 7 inches	224 feet 9 $1/_2$ inches
Discus:	138 feet 7 inches	164 feet 2 inches
1,500-meter run:	4 minutes 18 seconds	4 minutes 12.6 seconds